D1326036

First published in Great Britain in 2009 by Buster Books,
an imprint of Michael O'Mara Books Limited,
9 Lion Yard, Tremadoc Road, London SW4 7NQ

Written by Jo Bourne and Matthew Rake
Illustrated by Lyn Stone/The Art Agency
Shutterstock Images on pages 18, 19, 36, 42, 46, 48, 49
Created and produced by Toucan Books
3rd Floor, 89 Charterhouse Street, London EC1M 6HR
Produced by Joanne Rooke
Cover design by Zoe Quayle (from a design by www.blacksheep-uk.com)
Cover illustration by Paul Moran

A CIP catalogue record for this book is available from the British Library

ISBN: 978-1-906082-56-7

2 4 6 8 10 9 7 5 3 1

www.mombooks.com/busterbooks

Printed and bound in Italy by Rotolito Lombarda

Papers used by Buster Books are natural, recyclable products made from wood grown in sustainable forests. The manufacturing processes conform to the environmental regulations of the country of origin.

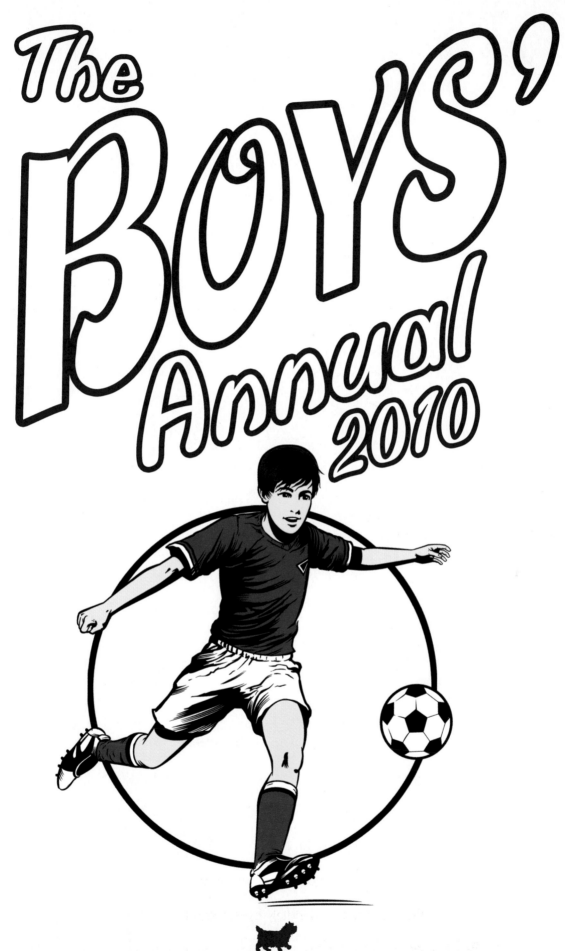

The BOYS' Annual 2010

Buster Books

CONTENTS

Amazing Stories

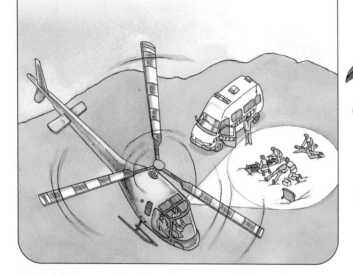

Cool Cooking

Fun Things to Do

Did You Know

Could You Avoid The Pirates' Plank?

Ahoy … me hearties! You've been kidnapped by pirates. Can you save your skin with your cabin-boy charm, or will you walk the plank?

1. The Captain tells you to salute the Jolly Roger. What do you do?

A) Salute the Captain.
B) Salute the skull and crossbones flag.
C) Salute the first mate – he looks like a happy chappie.

2. You are ordered to swab the poop deck, splice the main brace, then make fast to the bilge. What do you do?

A) Mop the floor above the Captain's quarters, mend the rigging, then run down to the bottom of the ship.
B) Clean the Captain's toilet, sprinkle the ropes with salt and pepper, then run to the back of the ship.
C) Throw seawater down the shipmates' loos, tie the first mate to the mast and then run to the smelliest crewman you can find.

3. The first mate offers you a wormy ship's biscuit. It's a special pirate treat. What do you do?

A) Say 'No thanks, I'm a vegetarian.'
B) Eat it all. You can't risk offending him.
C) Take a small bite, then distract the mate and slip some in your pocket and use it later to bribe his monkey.

4. You are sent to the crow's nest at the top of the mast. What do you do when you get there?
A) Fetch eggs for the Captain's lunch.
B) Watch out for crows and seagulls.
C) Look out for other ships.

DID YOU KNOW?

- The 'Jolly Roger' is the name given to the skull and crossbones flag.
- The 'poop deck' is the deck above the Captain's cabin, at the rear of the ship.
- The 'main brace' is the thickest part of the rigging and is made of rope. If this gets damaged it has to be 'spliced', which means mended.
- The 'bilge' is the lowest, dirtiest part of the ship.

5. Another pirate ship attacks and the pirates come aboard to fight. You don't have a weapon. What do you do?

A) Try to stay out of the action – if the other crew wins you'll want to join them. There's no point hanging around with a bunch of losers.

B) Try to stay hidden in the bilge – after all, you don't want to get hurt.

C) Fight with anything you can lay your hands on – bottles of rum, the first mate's monkey, even the Captain's parrot.

6. Your crew have won the fight, taken prisoners, sung shanties and downed bottles of rum. Now they're all snoring. You see the other ship's cabin boy escape his ties, and make for a rowing boat to take him back to his empty ship. What do you do?

A) Wake the Captain. There'll be no prisoners escaping on your watch.

B) Follow him. You might be able to persuade him to row you to the nearest shore.

C) Follow him. Once you're safe aboard the other ship you can take over and become Captain yourself.

Now add up your score:

1.	A=2	B=3	C=1
2.	A=3	B=2	C=1
3.	A=1	B=2	C=3
4.	A=1	B=2	C=3
5.	A=3	B=1	C=2
6.	A=2	B=1	C=3

Turn to page 60 to find out whether you'd qualify as a lousy landlubber or a perfect pirate.

Talk Like A Pirate

International 'Talk Like A Pirate Day' is held every year on the 19th of September, during which you get to talk like a pirate all day. If you've got pirattitude, then here are some key words and phrases. If in doubt, just say 'Arrr'.

Ahoy, me hearties – 'Hello'
Aye Aye – 'Yes, yes'
Avast – 'Stop that!' or 'Hey'
Shiver me timbers – An expression of surprise
Smartly – 'Hurry up'

Secret Stash

Got something you want to hide? Here are two secret stashes you can make to keep things safe from prying parents, busybody brothers and super-sneaky sisters.

Secret Stash Box

YOU WILL NEED:

A shoebox, or similar
4 empty matchboxes
PVA glue
Cardboard
A ruler

Scissors
Black paint
A paintbrush
Black thread
Sticky tape

STEP 1

Inside the box, glue a matchbox into each of the bottom corners.

STEP 2

Measure the dimension of the bottom of the shoebox, then cut a piece of cardboard to fit snugly inside. This will sit on top of the matchboxes and make the false bottom.

STEP 3

Paint the inside of the box, and the piece of card, black. Leave to dry.

Glue the matchboxes on their sides, so you have a 4-cm-high compartment.

STEP 4

Cut a length of black thread 1½ times the length of the box. Tape one end to the underside of the false bottom, in the middle and near the edge (see below). Then, tape the other end to the opposite side.

STEP 5

Holding the black thread, drop the false bottom into place on top of the matchboxes. To lift it out again, just pull on the thread – it's a nearly invisible handle.

Put some stuff on top of the false bottom to keep your secret compartment hidden.

Secret Stash Jar

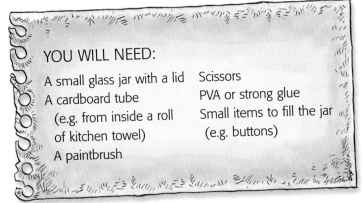

YOU WILL NEED:

A small glass jar with a lid

A cardboard tube
(e.g. from inside a roll
of kitchen towel)

A paintbrush

Scissors

PVA or strong glue

Small items to fill the jar
(e.g. buttons)

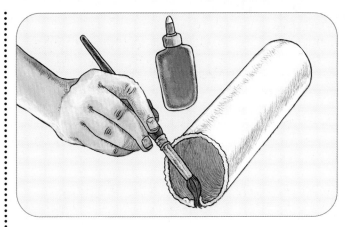

STEP 2

Using a brush, spread a generous amount of glue around the bottom edge of the tube.

STEP 1

Cut the cardboard tube so it is slightly shorter than the height of the inside of the jar.

STEP 3

Slide the tube into the jar – with the glued edge facing down – and press it into place in the centre of the jar. Leave to dry.

STEP 4

Fill the outer ring, so that the central tube is hidden from view. Use buttons, paper clips, nuts and bolts, or anything else you can think of.

STEP 5

Stash your secrets in the hidden tube, then screw the lid back on to keep them safe.

TOP TIP
To disguise your tube even more, paint it the same colour as the contents of the jar, e.g. silver-grey if you're storing nuts and bolts in it.

Putting boring stuff like paper clips in the jar means no one will want to open it.

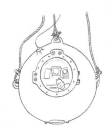

Dive Into The Deep

Comb the deep sea and spot the ten differences between these two pictures. All the answers are on page 60. You'd need a mini-submarine to get to these depths safely – a diver would be crushed by the pressure of the water above.

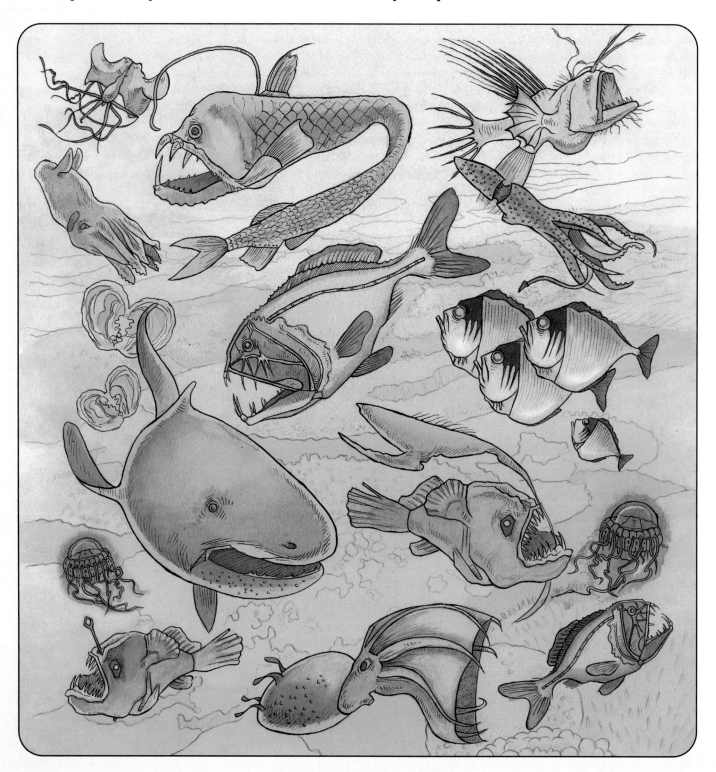

Can you match the fish descriptions with the illustrations? Answers on page 60.

1. Big, rubbery-lipped megamouth shark.
2. Poisonous, dome-headed jelly fish.
3. Leggy, pink deep-sea squid.
4. Flat, shiny-bodied hatchetfish.
5. Fanged, silvery-purple viperfish.
6. Yellow, long-spined anglerfish.

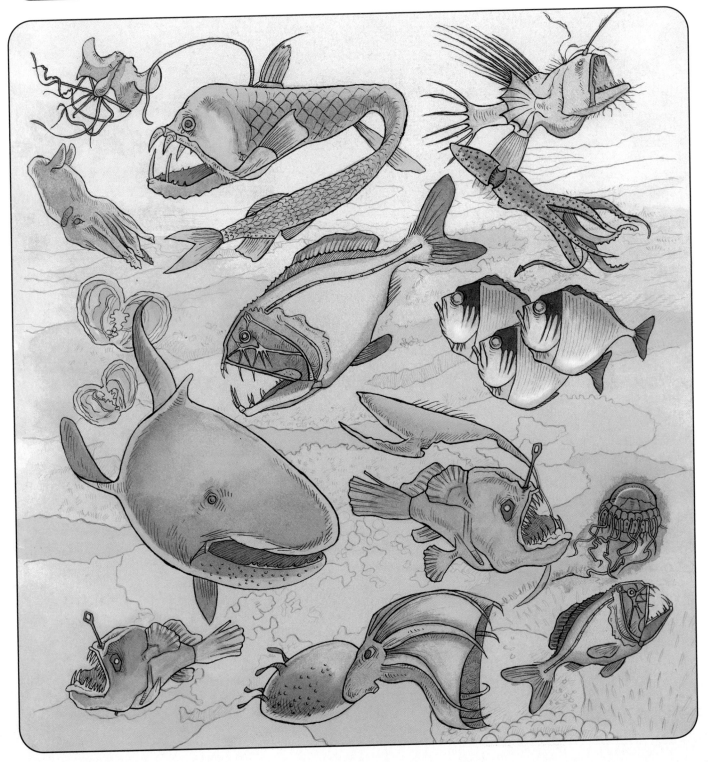

WOW! MAGGIE'S HAD PUPPIES ... AND LOOK AT ALL THAT MONEY.

GUYS, I'VE FOUND THE STOLEN MONEY. WE'D BETTER CALL THE POLICE.

I CAN'T THANK YOU BOYS ENOUGH. I DON'T KNOW WHAT I'D HAVE DONE WITHOUT MAGGIE.

WE'D LIKE TO THANK YOU BOYS, TOO.

I WON'T SIGN THE CONTRACT FOR ANOTHER WEEK - THAT GIVES YOU ALL THE TIME YOU WANT TO PRACTISE FOR YOUR BIG DAY.

WITH THE FINGERPRINTS ON THE BANKNOTES, WE'LL CATCH THOSE CRIMINALS IN NO TIME.

AT THE SKATEBOARDING CHAMPIONSHIP ...

A SUPERB FINALE THERE FROM KURT, HARRY, JOSH AND BILL.

AND FOR ALL YOU CHAMPIONS, WORK STARTS ON THE NEW SKATEBOARD PARK AT THE COMMUNITY CENTRE NEXT WEEK.

WOW, WE WON!

Mighty Maze

Can you pick the right path around the skate park to create the winning routine? You need to begin at the START and find your route to the FINISH. Answer on page 60.

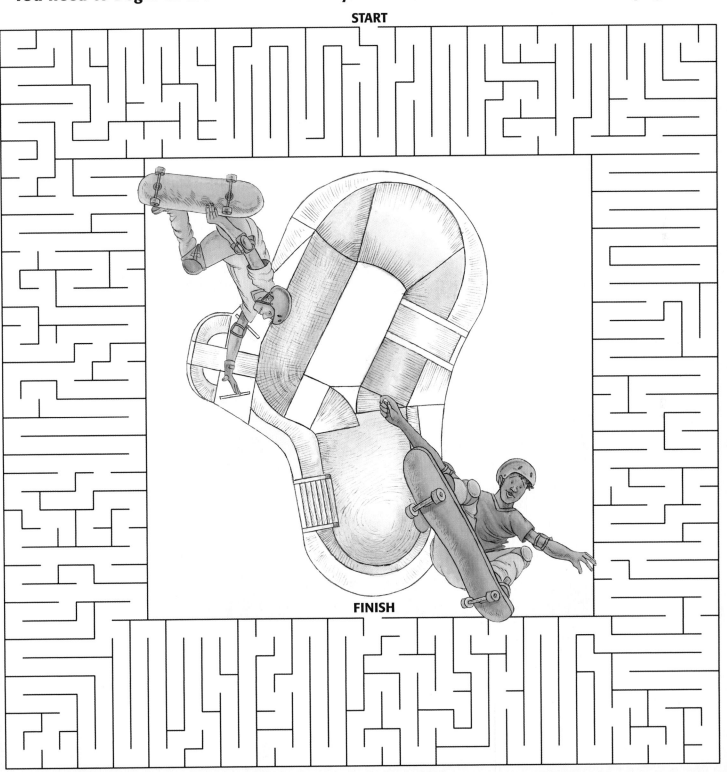

START

FINISH

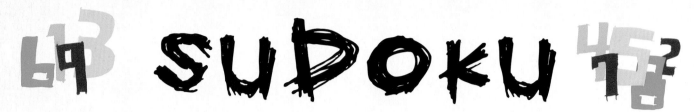

SUDOKU

Sudoku is a cool kind of number puzzle that started in Japan. To solve Sudoku puzzles you don't need to be good at maths – you just need to think logically. So come on brainiacs, let's see what you are made of. Answers on page 61.

THE RULES ARE SIMPLE

Below is a Sudoku puzzle grid. There are some numbers already in the grid. To fill the empty squares, you need to add the numbers 1, 2, 3 and 4, but you can only have one of each in any column (one is shown in red), row (blue), and box (yellow).

3.		**4**	
2			
			4
4		**3**	**1**

TOP TIP

1. Look for the column, or row, or box with the most numbers in – and work out that bit of the puzzle first.

2. Look for the number that is used most. Then work out where that number can be placed in the rest of the Sudoku puzzle. Remember, each number has to appear in each column, each row and each box.

BEGINNER

How to get started: The bottom-right box contains three numbers – so add the fourth number. Now the third column from the left and the bottom row have only one number missing. Add them. The top-left box has two numbers missing – 1 and 4. There's already a 4 in the top row, so the empty square at the top of the second column can't take a 4. Can you carry on?

3		**4**	
2			
			4
4		**3**	**1**

Keep a record of how long you take to do a puzzle. You will see that you get faster.

DID YOU KNOW?

- Sudoku was invented by a man called Howard Garns from the USA, in 1979. He called the puzzle 'Number Place'.
- A Japanese company called 'Nikoli' began publishing the puzzles in 1986. They called it Sudoku, which means 'single number' in Japanese.
- The first World Sudoku Championship was held in Italy in 2006.

MEDIUM

How to get started: The first and fourth columns in the grid below have got two numbers already positioned – start by getting the third and fourth numbers in each column. Good luck!

KILLER

How to get started: Yikes – each column, row and box has only one number in it. However, the number 4 is repeated twice – start by seeing if you can place the other two 4s.

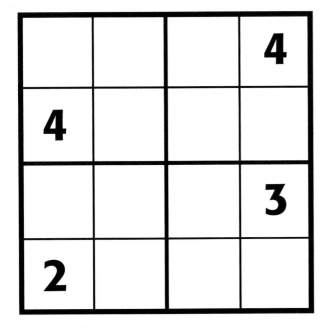

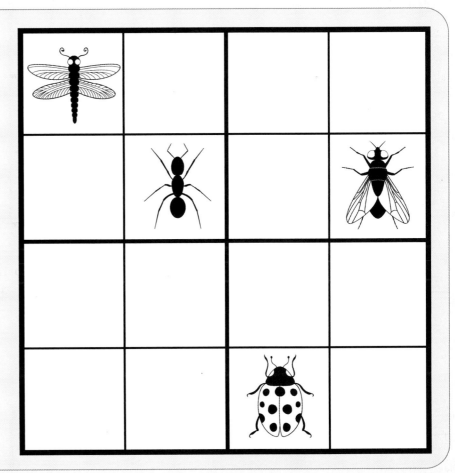

INSECT SUDOKU

Here is a puzzle that will really bug you. The numbers have been replaced by dragonflies, ants, flies and ladybirds. The aim of the game, however, is the same – each column, row and box has to have one of each insect.

How to get started:
Start with the top-left box – it needs a fly and a ladybird and there's already a fly in the second row.

CONFIDENTIAL

IS THERE ANYBODY OUT THERE?

Some scientists think there might be life elsewhere in the universe, and four million Americans think they have encountered aliens. What's the truth?

MYSTERY LIGHTS

Strange lights in the sky have been seen for centuries. In medieval times, people believed they were caused by dragons breathing fire from their nostrils.

No one called these unexplained lights 'flying saucers' until 1947, when a pilot named Kenneth Arnold was sent on a mission to find a lost plane in north-western America. He reported seeing nine glittering discs flying in a formation above him. A newspaper published his story, along with a dramatic drawing. The public were captivated. Soon, many more people, including other pilots, came forward to say they, too, had seen strange flying objects. It was at this point that the United States Air Force named the unexplained lights 'Unidentified Flying Objects', or UFOs for short. They were objects which science or common sense just couldn't explain.

Then one science magazine called *True* suggested that UFOs were craft from space, flown by beings from another world. This became the favourite explanation.

EXTRA- TERRESTRIAL VISITORS

People began to come forward to say they had met alien visitors and had been taken up into the UFOs, sometimes against their will. But no evidence of these alien encounters was ever found.

The same year, 1947, something fell to Earth at a place called Roswell in the New Mexico desert. Official reports said it was a weather balloon. However, many people still believe that it was a UFO, and that aliens were found inside it and were studied by scientists. These aliens were named 'greys' and were thought to look a bit like ET, the loveable alien from the movie of the same name.

Nowadays, we have simpler explanations for strange lights in the sky. They might be 'ball' lightning (like regular lightning but round), meteors (dust from comets that creates a flash as it burns up in the Earth's atmosphere), the glowing planet Venus, or weather balloons.

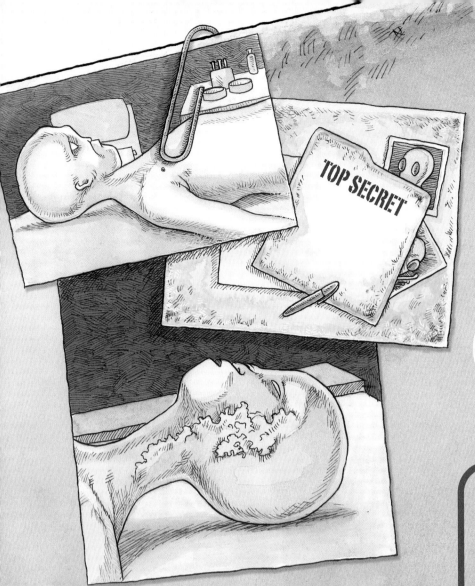

ALIEN AUTOPSY
In the 1990s, a man named Ray Santilli produced a piece of film that he claimed showed the body of a dead alien found near Roswell being examined. Although Santilli admitted the film was a fake in 2006, he still insisted the alien had existed and the autopsy had taken place.

JOKE TIME
Q. What do you call a spaceship with a faulty air-conditioning unit?
A. A frying saucer!

THE TRUTH ABOUT CROP CIRCLES
Strange circles and geometric patterns began to appear in the fields of southwest England in the 1980s. Some people blamed these areas of flattened corn on whirlwinds, or mad sheep and rabbits. However, a few people believed that they were the work of aliens, trying to communicate with earthlings by creating geometric shapes.

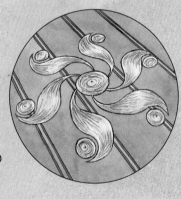

It turned out that the patterns, known as crop circles, were elaborate hoaxes. Groups of people were going out at night and flattening the crops themselves. Some burned the patterns into fields and others cut them into the ground.

But that's not the end of the story. On their nightly missions, some of the circle-makers began to report strange events occurring in the fields. One person even admitted that he had no idea why he made the circles, and that perhaps he was being controlled by aliens … it seems that the story has come full circle!

SETI
Scientists are hard at work looking for alien life in the universe. An organisation called SETI, which stands for Search for Extraterrestrial Intelligence, uses giant telescopes to look for them. So far, they haven't found anything.

If there are aliens out there, they may know about us. In 1974, US scientists beamed a three-minute message into space. It included a picture of humans and information about life in our solar system. Moreover, TV, radio and radar signals generated on Earth have been bouncing off into space for 50 years. The first 50-year-old signals are just now reaching 1,000 of the closest stars to our solar system. So maybe aliens are laughing at the jokes in the earliest TV shows right now.

Alien Hands

Here's a handy idea for frightening your friends – a pair of alien mitts. They're easy to make, seriously spooky and, literally, out of this world.

YOU WILL NEED:
A sheet of stiff cardboard
2 pieces of dowel
  (30 cm long) or
  2 pencils
Newspaper
A pen
Scissors
Sticky tape
PVA glue
A spatula
A paintbrush
Green acrylic paint

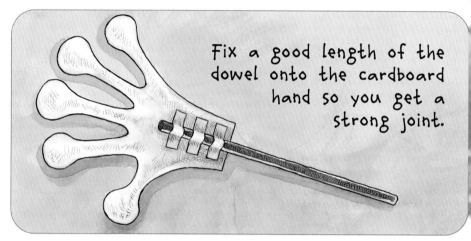

Fix a good length of the dowel onto the cardboard hand so you get a strong joint.

STEP 1
Draw two alien hand-shapes onto card. Make the fingers long and skinny with round blobs at the end for an extra-weird alien look. Cut the hands out.

STEP 2
Use sticky tape to fix a dowel stick, or pencil, securely to one side of each cardboard hand.

STEP 3
Scrunch newspaper into small balls, then apply glue to the base of each ball with the spatula and stick onto the cardboard. Repeat until both sides of each hand are covered.

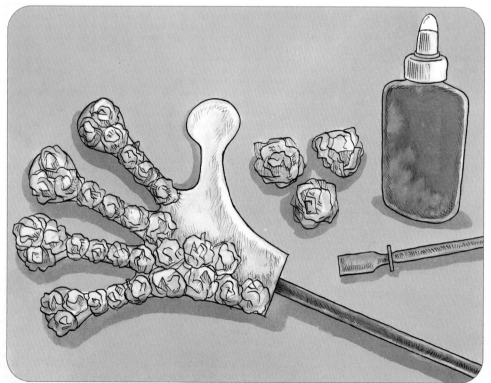

Scrunch the newspaper tightly and glue it down firmly.

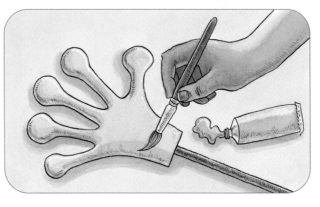

STEP 4

Tear more newspaper into strips and paste them onto each hand, covering all of the scrunched balls of newspaper. Overlap the strips as you stick them down and wrap them around the edges of each hand.

STEP 5

When the glue is completely dry, brush on two coats of acrylic paint. You can either make them plain, or paint on strange, alien-ish patterns (green hands with red spots look good).

TOP TIP

Try using glow-in-the-dark paint for a super-spooky finish. Then you can scare people in the dark.

If your sleeves are a bit too long, it's even better for hiding your real hands.

WHEN THEY ARE FINISHED

To use the hands, slip on a sweater or jacket with long sleeves. Hold one stick in each of your real hands, then shake your sleeves down so only the alien hands are sticking out of the end of each sleeve. Creepy!

Rescue In The Snow

A fall of snow is a recipe for fun and games. But sometimes snowy weather brings danger, and with it daring acts of rescue – as these two true stories show.

Saved From A Snowy Prison

In December 2008, shortly before Christmas, 21-year-old Logan Jeck was walking in the mountains above the village of McBride, British Columbia, Canada. He was on his way to pick up a couple of tourist snowmobiles, when he came across two horses buried deep in the snow – starving, frozen and very ill.

The snow was so deep, it was impossible to lead the horses back to safety. He could only hope they would survive the night.

Rescue Mission

Logan returned with his sister the next day with a bale of hay and a rifle. Their father was a horseman, and said that if the horses were too ill to eat the hay it was kinder to put them down. Logan put the hay on the ground, and the horses began eating it eagerly. Now he knew he had to try and get the horses off the mountain to safety. But how was he going to do that?

Back in the village, people were making plans. They considered air lifting the horses by helicopter, dragging them out on sleds, or making special snowshoes so the horses could walk without sinking. However, there was only one real solution – dig a long passage through the snow so the horses could walk the one-kilometre distance back to the village.

With no time to waste, the villagers abandoned their Christmas preparations and began the hard job of digging a corridor through the metre-high snowdrifts. The horses now had blankets, food and warmth from small fires, but they were weak, and could not survive much longer. The people of McBride had to dig fast.

'The snow was so deep, it was impossible to lead the horses back to safety.'

A Race Against Time

The villagers shovelled for days. After almost a week of effort – and just two days before Christmas – the passage was finished. The horses were led on the seven-hour trek through the narrow snow corridor, across frozen tracks to the safety of a warm, dry stable.

For many of the McBride villagers, there were no Christmas presents that year – they had been too busy digging. However, they all agreed that saving the horses was the best present they'd ever had.

Drama At Devil's Dyke

When snow started to fall in England in February 2008, three Brighton boys thought they were in for some fun. As night fell, they headed off with their sledges to Devil's Dyke – a steep V-shaped valley on the South Downs.

The snow was perfect and the dark added to their excitement. The boys all jumped into one sledge and sped down the hill. Unfortunately for them, the fun was short-lived. Their sledge hit a rock, and the teenagers were catapulted into the bottom of the valley.

Call For Help

Friends who had joined them on the slope watched in horror. They saw that the boys were unable to move, and quickly called for help. In no time, a police helicopter flew in. It pinpointed the boys' position, but couldn't land in the narrow valley, and no ambulance could reach them from the snow-covered hilltop road above. This was serious. With no help, the boys would be in danger of hypothermia.

The Emergency Plan

While their friends kept the boys warm and awake, the rescue team made a plan. The police helicopter flew back to the road and made contact with an ambulance, instructing it to begin the slow and bumpy journey of nearly a mile in the dark. The helicopter then hovered above the ground and lit the route for the ambulance using its powerful searchlight. This guided the ambulance through fields and round hidden obstacles in the snow.

When the ambulance arrived, it was clear the boys' injuries were serious. One had a fractured pelvis, one had broken his shoulder, while the third had broken ribs and had internal bleeding. The crew assessed the injuries in the bright light of the police helicopter, then drove the boys off the slope and into a waiting hospital vehicle.

The boys recovered well, thanks to their speedy rescue, but they vowed to stick to less extreme sports next time snow fell on the steep slopes of Devil's Dyke.

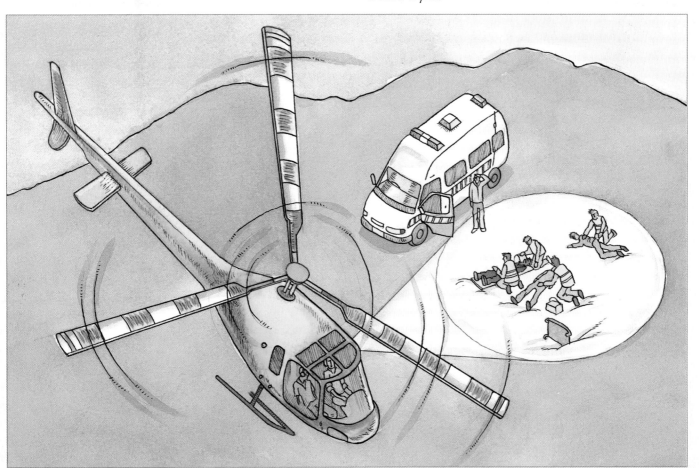

Pizza Party

This recipe takes minutes to make, and as soon as it comes off the grill, you just know that everyone will want a 'pizza' the action.

INGREDIENTS:

Pizza base:
1 large French stick

Basic topping:
150 g jar tomato sauce
250 g mozzarella cheese

Extra toppings:
thinly sliced onion,
sliced pepperoni,
diced yellow or red
  peppers,
chopped ham,
pineapple pieces, and
pitted olives

STEP 3
Spread the toasted side of the bread with the tomato sauce and add a selection of extra toppings.

For a really juicy pizza, lay the sauce on thick.

STEP 1
Carefully cut the French stick in half, then split in two lengthways. (It's a good idea to ask an adult to help you when using a sharp knife.)

STEP 2
Toast the cut sides facing upwards under a preheated grill, on a medium heat, until pale golden brown.

STEP 4
Grate the mozzarella cheese and arrange on top of the pizza. Place under the grill and cook until the cheese melts. Allow to cool for a few moments before serving.

Warning: Take extra care when using knives and remember to use oven gloves when placing the pizzas under the grill.

Pizza Names
Which of the pizzas shown here would you get if you ordered:
a) Pepperoni   **b)** Margarita
c) Funghi   **d)** Hawaiian?
Answers on page 61.

1   **2**   **3**   **4**

Make A Cool Camp

Tarpaulins, or tarps, are square sheets of waterproof nylon or plastic with small holes around the edges. They're cheap, light and will give you shelter in an instant.

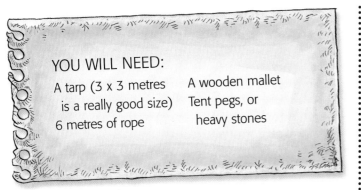

YOU WILL NEED:

A tarp (3 x 3 metres is a really good size)

6 metres of rope

A wooden mallet

Tent pegs, or heavy stones

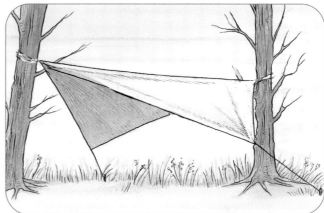

A Flying Tarp

This is the real bushman's shelter. Tie opposite corners to two trees, as high as you can. Peg the two other corners to the ground, using about a metre of rope, as far away as the rope allows (see above). This gives you a large space to shelter from the sun or rain.

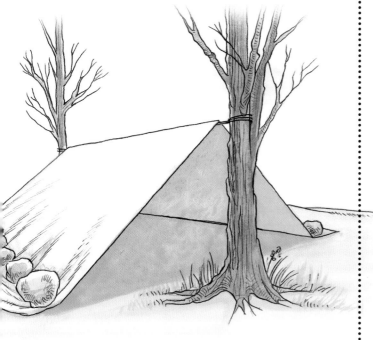

Camouflage Ideas

Look around for what you can use as camouflage – your tent needs to blend in with its surroundings. If you're in a wood, heap dead leaves, or twigs, onto the tarp to disguise your shelter.

A Two-Tree Tarp

Look for two trees slightly further apart than the length of your tarp, with some flat ground in between. Tie a length of rope from one tree to another, about a metre off the ground. Make sure the rope is taut and straight. Throw the tarp over the rope, then arrange it in a tent shape, pulling it tight and making sure there is an equal amount of tarp on each side of the rope. Peg it to the ground, or secure it with two rows of heavy stones.

Be a CONKER Conqueror

**Challenge your friends and family to a traditional game of conkers
– with these hints and tips, you're sure to be the champ.**

COLLECT AND PREPARE

1. Find a healthy chestnut tree, then look for fallen conkers. Make sure they're big, shiny and don't have holes in them.

2. Ask an adult to help you make a hole in the centre of the conker using a small hand-held drill.

3. Thread a 25-cm-long piece of string through the hole, and tie a big knot at the end.

**Warning:
Make sure you hold the conker out in front of you and be careful of your eyes and hands when playing.**

RULES OF THE GAME

1. Each player takes it in turns to strike their opponent's conker. The defending conker hangs still while the attacking conker thwacks it as hard as possible.

2. If one of the conkers comes off the string but doesn't break, the other player can try to jump on it. This is called a 'stampsie'.

3. If the strings get tangled, the first one to shout 'strings' takes the next shot.

TOP TIP
Rub handcream on your conker. It will make it softer and less likely to break when struck.

4. The player that smashes the other player's conker is the winner, and the winning conker is given a name (see below).

NAMING YOUR CONKER

NONE-ER A brand new conker.

ONE-ER A conker that breaks a none-er.

TWO-ER A conker that breaks a one-er or two none-ers.

SIX-ER A conker that breaks one none-er and one five-er.

(You get the idea …)

Popcorn Balls

**Yum … popcorn and marshmallows. That's one super-sweet snack.
You're going to have a ball making and eating these treats.**

INGREDIENTS:

4 tablespoon of sunflower or corn oil
100 g popping corn
50 g butter
200 g marshmallows

Warning: Ask an adult to help you heat up the popcorn mixture. Hot oil and sugar can burn you severely. Remember to use oven gloves when shaking the pan.

Keep stirring so you get a good, gooey gunge.

STEP 1

Heat half the oil in a large saucepan, then add half the popcorn. Cover with a lid and cook over a low heat until all the popcorn has popped. Shake the pan constantly.

STEP 3

Melt the butter in a small saucepan over a low heat. Once the butter has melted begin adding the marshmallows and cook gently, stirring until all the marshmallows have melted.

You want your popcorn shaken not stirred.

Carefully stir the popcorn into the marshmallow mixture to avoid crushing it.

STEP 2

When the popping has finished, remove from the heat. Leave the lid on for a minute or two and then transfer the popcorn to a warm bowl. Repeat steps one and two with the remaining popcorn.

STEP 4

Pour the marshmallow mixture over the popcorn and stir until well coated. Scoop out mounds of the popcorn, shape into balls and then place on an oiled baking sheet. Repeat until all the popcorn has been used. Allow the popcorn balls to set before serving.

HOW TO PLAY DODGEBALL

Dodgeball is a nonstop, all-action game, and it's masses of fun. Once you learn how to play, it's sure to become your favourite game. Grab your mates and get throwing.

WHAT YOU NEED

You need at least six players and two balls to play. Ideally, use as many balls as there are players – the more balls and people there are, the more chaotic fun you'll have. Only use lightweight foam balls. Don't use normal footballs – they are too heavy and someone could get hurt.

ON YOUR MARKS

Mark out a rectangular dodgeball court roughly 15 metres long and 10 metres wide. Mark a line across the width of the court at its midpoint – this is your 'centre line'. Now mark out two lines, about 1.5 metres either side of the centre line – these are your 'attack lines'. If you're in a playground, you can mark the court in chalk. In the park, use ropes or string to mark the boundaries.

Top Tips
Fastest First
Get your fastest players to grab the balls.

Throw Quickly
If you're holding a ball, you're a prime target. You'll be looking at who you can throw at – rather than who is aiming at you.

Stay Alert
Players who've been sent off have to retrieve stray balls and pass them back quickly. Your team's survival depends on it!

READY TO PLAY?

Place all the balls on the centre line. Each team starts behind their 'baseline', which is the line furthest away from the centre line. On the whistle, players must race to the balls, pick them up and take them behind their attack line. Players then throw the balls at the other team.

Scoring A Hit

A 'hit' is scored if a player manages to hit an opposition player's body without the ball bouncing on the ground first. It must hit that player below the head and have been thrown from behind the attack line. Any player hit like this is out, and must leave the court. If you hit someone in the face, it is a foul and you must leave the court.

Catching

If a player manages to catch a ball thrown at him, a player on his team who has been sent off can return to the game. Players must return in the same order in which they got sent off – so the first person out is the first person back.

Deflecting

If you are holding a ball, you can use it to deflect a thrown ball coming towards you. However, you're out if the ball hits any part of your body or makes you drop the ball you are holding.

Retrieving Balls

Players who've been sent off must retrieve balls that go out of play and place them on the centre line. If no players have been sent off, court players retrieve stray balls. This is the only time they can step outside off the court. If a player jumps out of the court to dodge a ball, he will be sent off.

Be Honourable

If you're hit, admit it and leave the court. Even if you have a referee, they won't be able to spot every hit. So all players need to be honest.

How To Win

Continue until you are all exhausted, or one team has no players left on court and loses.

DRAGON DODGEBALL

This is a circle-based variation of Dodgeball. Here's how to play:

Divide up into two teams of equal numbers. One team forms a large circle. The other team forms a chain or 'dragon', with each player holding the one in front around the waist. The dragon enters the circle. Look at your watch and start timing now. The players in the circle must aim the ball at the tail player in the dragon. When that person is hit, he exits from the circle and the next player on the tail is the target. Play until all players in the dragon have been hit. Then swap the teams. Keep a record of how long each team stayed in. The team whose dragon lasts the longest wins.

CURSE FROM THE GRAVE

A mummy is the preserved body of a dead person – and many people believe that mummies carry curses. Is this fact or fib? Read on and decide for yourself.

CURSE OF THE BOY KING

In 1922, the archaeologist Howard Carter made one of the greatest discoveries of the century – the tomb of Tutankhamun in Egypt.

The boy-king's mummy had lain undisturbed for more than 3,000 years and, as the press around the world received news of the wonderful treasures in the tomb, stories of bad luck and ancient curses began to circulate. The Egyptians inscribed curses on their tombs to ward off grave robbers.

The following year, as the slow, steady work on the tomb progressed, weird things started happening. Lord Carnarvon – the rich man who had paid for the tomb to be opened – fell ill in Cairo and died. At the moment of his death, all the lights went out in the city and back in England his dog howled inconsolably and died. Was this the curse at work? Many believed so.

Since then, the story of the curse has faded. There were common explanations for the events. Lord Carnarvon died from an infected mosquito bite – an unfortunate, but not mysterious incident. At that time, electricity was notoriously unreliable in Cairo and the lights went out all the time. As for the dog, that surely was a coincidence.

What's more, apart from Carnarvon, virtually all of the exploration team lived on for many years before dying of natural causes in old age. Howard Carter was around for 17 years after the tomb's opening.

When archaeologists found the wonderful treasures of Tutankhamun did they also curse themselves?

TERROR IN THE ICE

So, is the mummies' curse just a made-up story? It seemed so … until 1991, when two German walkers in the Alps came upon a body trapped in ice. The man, named Otzi after the valley in which he was found, turned out to be 5,300 years old. He was soon big news, and experts were employed to preserve his remains.

Then the deaths started. First Dr Rainer Henn, who examined Otzi's body, died in a car crash. Kurt Fritz, a mountaineer who helped recover Otzi's body, died in an avalanche. Rainer Hoelzl, a filmmaker, died of a mystery illness months after his film of Otzi was shown. Finally, one of the walkers, Helmut Simon, died in a blizzard just 200 kilometres from where he found the ice man. This looked like more than a coincidence, and the press recalled the Tutankhamun 'mummy curse'. Could the ice man be exerting his power from beyond the grave? It's up to you to decide.

In 1991, the body was found – and then some very strange things started happening.

Some 5,300 years ago, high up in the Alps, a man got caught in a blizzard and fell to his death.

JOKE TIME

Q. Where do mummies go for a swim?
A. The Dead Sea

DID YOU KNOW?

- The word 'mummy' has got nothing to do with mothers. It comes from 'mumiyah' – the Arabic word for the sticky oil used to preserve the bodies of the dead.
- Mummification in Ancient Egypt was not for the faint-hearted. Before the body was dried out and wrapped in bandages, the brain was removed.
- In 1995, two walkers in the Andes mountains in Peru came across a perfectly preserved mummy of a girl – nick-named Juanita or the 'Ice Maiden'. She had lived in the Ancient Inca civilization and had been encased in ice for 500 years. It was only when a nearby volcano erupted that the ice melted. Juanita had been frozen so well that even the food inside her stomach was preserved.

The Bubble-Gum God

Jack's brother, Ethan, was the coolest boy in school, but he was also a bit of a bully. Jack found a way to teach him a lesson, with the help of a spooky friend …

History Class

'Okay everyone, as tomorrow is our trip to the Roman villa, today's lesson will be on the Romans. The villa and the small temple in the grounds were built nearly two thousand years ago … Jack, please pay attention!'

Jack had been staring glumly out the window. His older brother, Ethan, was so mean. Last night he had hidden Jack's school bag – a favourite trick – and made him late. But everybody liked Ethan. He played football, he was in a band, his hair was cool. If only Jack could get even with him.

'The Romans went to the temple to pray,' the teacher went on. 'They also cursed people they didn't like.' He held up a picture of a small, dirty piece of metal with marks on it. 'This is a curse tablet. The Romans wrote their wishes – or curses – on soft sheets of lead, then left their problem for the gods to take care of.'

Jack was paying attention now. That's all it would take, he thought. A bit of tin foil and a ballpoint pen. He could make his own curse tablet, and leave it at the temple tomorrow, just like the Romans would have done. It had to be worth a go.

The Curse

The next day, Jack's class set off in a coach. When they arrived at the site, a guide greeted them and took them to see the temple. He explained that the Romans worshipped their gods by leaving offerings at the altar. He pointed at a pile of rubble, towards the back of the building. Unimpressed with the remains of the altar, the class filed out of the temple, but Jack hung behind. He crouched down, and hid his home-made curse tablet between some of the bricks.

'Are you sure you want to do that? They work, you know,' a voice said.

Jack turned round and saw a boy dressed in a Roman toga. He guessed he was one of the guides, though he looked a little young to have a job.

'Gods usually like a gift, too,' said the boy. 'Got a gift?'

'You seem to know a lot about it,' said Jack.

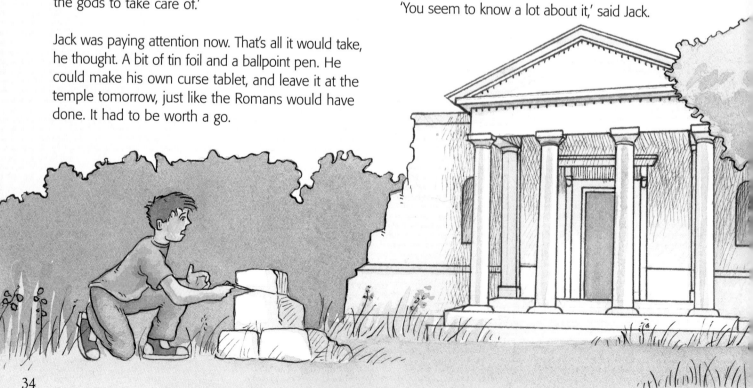

'Oh, I know all about the Romans,' replied the boy. 'Trust me.'

Jack felt in his pocket. 'I've got a packet of bubble gum I can leave. It's *Big Red Bubble-tastic*. Would the gods like that, d'you think?'

The boy smiled, 'Yes. That'll do.' Jack shut his eyes, wished for his brother to get a taste of his own medicine, and dropped the packet into the rubble.

'Well, I guess I'd better go.' The boy stood up and brushed the dust off his trousers. That was another thing – Ethan never got in trouble for getting dirty. He was much too vain about his appearance to get dirty.

'Good luck,' the boy called, as Jack made his way out of the temple. 'I'm sure things will be much better with your brother now.'

'That's odd,' thought Jack, as he approached the villa. 'Did I say anything about my brother?' He didn't have time to ponder. The teacher was waiting by the steps with his arms folded: 'Jack, last again! It's always you, isn't it?'

'Sorry,' said Jack. 'I was talking to the guide – the boy by the temple.'

The teacher peered over the field. 'What boy? Oh, never mind.' He hurried Jack up the steps to the villa.

The Revenge

When Jack got home there was no one in the house, but there was a note from his mother on the table, saying, 'Gone to the barbers with Ethan. Back soon.'

Jack got his books out ready to do his homework – for once he didn't have to listen to Ethan endlessly strumming the same two chords on his electric guitar.

After half an hour, he heard the key in the door. His mother came straight into the kitchen, while Ethan lurked in the doorway with his jacket hood up.

'I don't know how Ethan did it,' his mother said, crossly. 'He won't tell me. Bubble gum stuck in his hair – at the front and the back. I couldn't wash it out. I had to take him to the barbers to get it all cut off.' She pulled down Ethan's hood. He'd had a really, really, bad haircut. His cool fringe had been cut off, and he looked almost bald. Ethan scowled, whipped his hood back over his head, and ran upstairs.

'If you ask me it has got something to do with that group he plays in,' said his mother. 'I heard from Jim's mum, Mrs Murray, that they've formed a new group, "The Roman Gods' Revenge". Funny name for a band. Ethan doesn't seem interested. He says he isn't going to play music at all any more.'

Jack smiled to himself. His curse had come true – Ethan had suffered a really hair-raising experience! Then Jack thought of the boy at the villa. Was he actually a guide? Or a ghost? Or a god? Jack sat back and thought, 'He could be a great friend to have. I might ask Mum if she could drive me out to the villa again next weekend.'

MARVELLOUS MOTORS

See how quickly you can race through these puzzles. Answers on page 61.

WORD SCRAMBLE

Can you unscramble the following names of famous car makers. Write your answers in the grid. The word 'Ferrari' will help you get started.

1. ATIF
2. EULTRAN
3. FRDO
4. AURUBS
5. ELWKANVGOS
6. CEDEMSRE
7. INMI

1. F
2. E
3. R
4. R
5. A
6. R
7. I

CAR SILHOUETTE GAME

Match the dark shapes with the following cars.
1. Racing Car   **2.** Pick-up Truck   **3.** Supercar   **4.** Limousine.

JOKE TIME

Q. What do you call a man under a car?
A. Jack.

Q. What happened to the steel car with the steel motor and the steel wheels?
A. It steel wouldn't go!

Q. When is a car not a car?
A. When it turns into a garage.

WORDSEARCH

Can you find the names of the 20 cars in the grid? They may be written diagonally, forwards or backwards, as well as up and down. There is also the name of an Italian supercar with 11 letters. It begins with an 'L'.

ALFA ROMEO	DODGE	MAYBACH
ASTON MARTIN	FERRARI	MERCEDES
BENTLEY	FORD	MITSUBISHI
BMW	JAGUAR	PAGANI
BUGATTI	KOENIGSEGG	PORSCHE
CATERHAM	LOTUS	SPYKER
CHEVROLET	MASERATI	

```
P D M S H D B I W D B X F C H
P F H J U B Q I Q E K E A L C
T A L N I T R A M N O T S A M
G V G Z N S O S D T E E D M E
D G M A P A V L E R I H R B E
M L E Y N T K L H T H C O O C
Q A K S G I O A T M S S F R E
Y E S P G R M A B W I R Q G D
R E T E V I G O M S B O J H E
L Q L E R U N B J V U P A I S
R Y H T B A L E K L S I G N O
M C B F N F T G O S T L U I W
I R A R R E F I P K I A A B I
E N V M A Y B A C H M N R K R
E G D O D E A L F A R O M E O
```

COOL CAR FACTS

- The first car that people could actually buy was the Benz Patent Motorwagen. It had three wheels, no roof, and the engine was between the two back wheels. Basically, it was a jumped-up tricycle and it had to be pushed up steep hills. The first one was sold in 1888.

- There were no petrol stations in the early days of motoring. You had to fill your car with a cleaning product sold at chemists.

- The American Gary Gabelich was the first person in history to hit 1,000 km/h. His rocket-powered car was called 'Blue Flame'.

- David Beckham has owned Ferraris, Lamborghinis and Bentleys – but his first car was a Ford Escort.

- Manufacturers are developing cars that run on air. Seriously! You use a pump to compress the air in a tank inside the car. When the air expands, it powers the car.

MYTH BUSTERS

Want to become a real dino-buff? Here are some common beliefs about dinosaurs. Let's get to the bottom of whether they are fact or fiction.

☛ **Dinosaurs once ruled the world, living on land, in the air and in the sea.**

Not quite true. Flying reptiles called pterosaurs flew in the air, with wings made of skin. Other reptiles lived in the water, such as ichthyosaurs (who looked like dolphins) and mosasaurs (who looked like snakes with flippers). The creatures we call dinosaurs did not fly or live in water, they only ruled the land.

JOKE TIME

Q. What do you call a plated, spiky dinosaur when he is asleep?
A. Stegosnorus!

REMEMBER THIS!
- ALL DINOSAURS WERE REPTILES, BUT NOT ALL REPTILES WERE DINOSAURS.
- DINOSAURS COULD WALK UPRIGHT, BUT LIZARDS ONLY CRAWL.

☛ **Dinosaurs lived in prehistoric swamps.**

Well, some dinosaurs lived in swamps – because they were full of tasty food, such as turtles, eggs and plant life. However, many dinosaurs stood upright on small, pointy feet like those birds have – and they were definitely not designed for walking through sticky, swampy water.

In fact, dinosaurs lived in all sorts of habitats – including deserts. Some dinosaurs even lived in Antarctica. In the dinosaur era, Antarctica wasn't as cold as it is now, but it was still a pretty chilly place to live.

This is a **Tyrannosaurus Rex**. Most people know T-Rex was a vicious predator and hunter. But it was also a 'scavenger' which means it used its great sense of smell to lead it to dinosaurs and other creatures which were already dead, and then it fed off their bodies. Many predators alive today do this, including sharks and lions.

☞ **Birds are descended from dinosaurs.**
True. Birds evolved from a group of dinosaurs called theropods. Most scientists think that theropods were warm-blooded, like modern birds are, and many small theropods had skeletons very like those of birds. Some of these small theropods developed feathers from their scales. Why this happened is a mystery, but fossils prove that it did happen. Over time, feathers developed enough to allow their owners to fly. These creatures were no longer feathered dinosaurs but what we would now call birds.

This dinosaur is **Caudipteryx**. It was an unusual mix of reptile and bird. Caudipteryx didn't fly, but it had feathers and small wings. Its long legs probably meant it could run quite fast.

☞ **All the dinosaurs died when a massive asteroid hit the Earth 65 million years ago.**
Scientists are still debating why dinosaurs died out. Off the coast of Mexico there is a huge dent in the seafloor, called the Chicxulub Crater. It was caused by a giant asteroid that many scientists think hit the Earth and killed 70% of life on the planet. Life forms which weren't near the impact were probably wiped out by the tidal waves, acid rain and huge dust clouds that followed. Here are some other theories:

· **Attacks from space.** It may not have been an asteroid that wiped out the dinosaurs, but a massive comet hitting the Earth, or the radiation from an exploding star.

· **Volcanic explosion.** Volcanic eruptions in India may have blocked out the sun with dust and gas clouds, causing many plants to die, reducing the dinosaurs' food.

· **Destroyed by disease.** Biting insects carried diseases which they may have passed on to the dinosaurs.

· **Rise of the mammals.** As mammals began to thrive, they may have eaten all the dinosaurs' eggs.

Titanosaurs, like this one, roamed the world just before dinosaurs became extinct, living from 90 million years ago to 65 million years ago. They weighed up to 100 tonnes.

DID YOU KNOW?

· When a dinosaur bone was found in 1676, Oxford University professor Robert Plot thought it was the thigh bone of a giant human!
· The early dinosaur hunter Richard Owen came up with the word 'dinosaur' in 1842. It comes from Greek and means 'terrible lizard'.
· The Stegosaurus used its big, spiky tail as a weapon, swinging it like a club to injure carnivorous predators.

Fake Arm Cast

Do you want some sympathy from your mates, or maybe you just want to get out of games? Here's how to make a fake arm cast that will fool everyone.

YOU WILL NEED:

Cardboard (an empty cereal box will do)

Scissors

Sticky tape

Cotton wool

PVA glue

A spatula

Old newspapers

Wallpaper paste

An old, unwanted pair of tights (nylon tights, rather than woolly or patterned ones)

White paint

A paintbrush

STEP 3

Roll some cotton wool into balls, then glue a layer of these onto the outside of the tube.

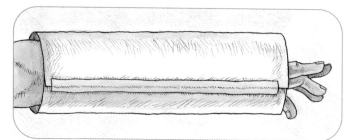

STEP 1

Cut a piece of thin cardboard and curve it around your arm. Overlap the edges, then tape it into place to create a cardboard tube that fits snugly around your arm.

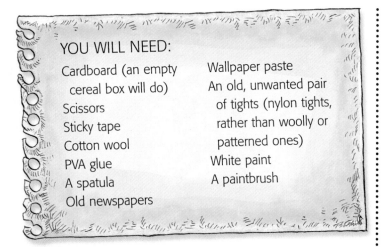

STEP 2

Cut out a hole near one end for your thumb to go through.

STEP 4

Tear newspaper into strips and glue it onto the cotton wool. Overlap the strips as you stick them down, to create a smooth layer around the tube. Then brush on a layer of wallpaper paste. Leave to dry completely.

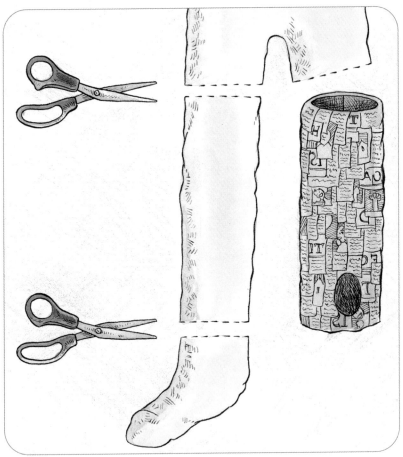

Always ask your mum or sister before you start cutting up their tights.

TOP TIP

Get your friends to write get well messages and autographs all over your cast (or fake it and do them yourself), for added effect.

STEP 5

Cut off one of the legs from a pair of tights. Trim it to the right length – it has to fit neatly over and around the edges of the tube. Cut a hole around the thumb hole. Stick this in place, then cover with another layer of wallpaper paste.

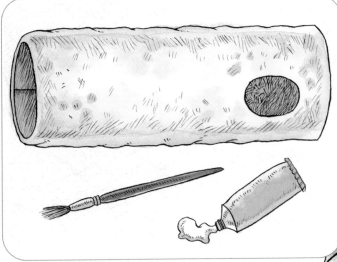

STEP 6

Leave the wallpaper paste to dry completely. Clean your brush and apply one or two coats of white paint.

41

COOL CARD TRICKS

All you need is a pack of cards and some time to practise. These tricks never fail!

PSYCHIC CARD

Convince a friend you can read his mind by guessing the card he is thinking of.

Skills Required: A good memory.

How To Do It

Deal four rows of three cards, with the red and black cards arranged in the pattern shown below. (It doesn't matter which red or black cards you use.)

To make this trick convincing, when your friends aren't looking, fix the order of the top 12 cards of the pack so you can deal them in the correct pattern. From the top card, they must be black, red, black, black, red, red, red, red, black, red, black, black.

Get your friend to secretly choose one of the **BLACK** cards (but remind him not to point to the card). Now tell him to make the following moves in his head. (Try to learn these moves by heart so you don't have to keep looking at this book.)

1. Ask your friend to move UP or DOWN to the nearest **RED** card.
2. Now, ask him to move LEFT or RIGHT to the nearest **BLACK** card.
3. Ask your friend to move DIAGONALLY to the nearest **RED** card.
4. Finally, ask him to move UP or DOWN to the nearest **BLACK** card and concentrate on that card.

No matter which card your friend initially chose, the card he ends up concentrating on will be the middle card on the bottom row. Pretend that you have read his mind and point to that card. You are psychic!

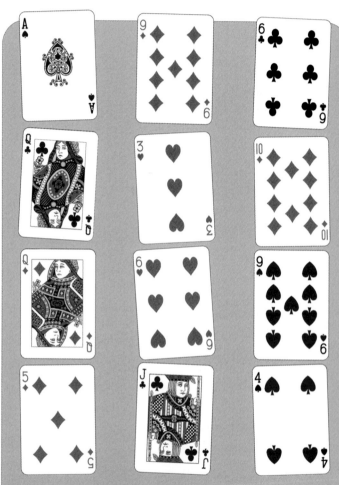

Here's an example …
Using the cards above, if the first card your friend picks is a queen of clubs, they will make the following moves:

1. Queen of clubs down to queen of diamonds.
2. Queen of diamonds across to nine of spades.
3. Nine of spades diagonally up to three of hearts.
4. Three of hearts down to jack of clubs.

When you come to reveal the jack of clubs, add some drama to the trick by pretending to concentrate really hard on the cards for, say, 15 seconds and then pick out the card.

MAGIC NUMBERS

In the 'Magic Numbers' trick, you will 'magically' be able to guess the numbers on the cards your friend has picked. It'll seem like magic – but it's really just maths.

Skills required: Basic arithmetic.

How To Do It

Remove all the tens, jacks, queens and kings from the pack. Keep the aces – they count as one.

1. Ask your friend to shuffle the pack and give it to you. Hold the cards face down in a fan, and get him to take a card without showing it to you. Tell your friend to remember the number of the card and put it back in the pack.

2. Now ask him to:
   a. Double the card's number.
   b. Add five to the total.
   c. Multiply the total by five.

3. Tell him to remember the final result. Now ask him to pick another card and add its number to the total. (The maths is not as hard as it seems – but use a pencil and paper if you need to.)

4. Ask them to tell you the final number. Subtract **25** from this number in your head. The two digits that make up the final total will be the numbers on the two cards your friend selected from your pack.

Here's an example …
Here's an example so you can see it works:
If the first card chosen is a five, doubling it makes ten. Adding five makes 15. Multiplying by five makes 75. Say the second card your friend chooses is an eight. He must add 75 to eight, which to make 83. You simply subtract 25 from the 83 – which makes **58**. Five and eight are therefore the numbers on the cards.

FLASH FINGERS

Using your 'flash fingers', you will be able to guess the card your friend has chosen. Practice makes perfect for this trick – because it relies on sleight of hand.

Skills Required: Nimble fingers.

How To Do It

Collect the cards into a single pile and make sure you know what the bottom card is. (You can do this easily by shuffling the cards and glancing at the bottom when you've finished.)

1. Hold the pack of cards face down in your left hand between your fingers and thumb.

2. Put the fingers of your right hand on top of the pack and the thumb on the bottom. Your right hand should now look as if it is going to pull the whole deck out of your left hand.

3. Using the fingers of your right hand, slide the cards at the top of the pack backwards, one by one. Ask your friend to stop you at any time.

4. Pull off the cards on top of the pack that you have moved backwards. At the same time, press your thumb on the bottom card and pull it away from the pack at the same time. This works best if you pull the bottom card out gradually as you slide back the top cards.

5. Now hold your right hand up so your friend can see the bottom card, but make sure you can't see it. (You don't need to see it because you already know what

it is.) Pretend to concentrate really hard – press the pack to your forehead in a dramatic way. Then announce what card your friend chose with confidence.

Make It Your Room

Want some hassle-free time in your own room? Try making this 'Keep Out!' sign. Once you've hung it up, use the peace and quiet to make this super-cool photo cube.

'Keep Out!' Sign

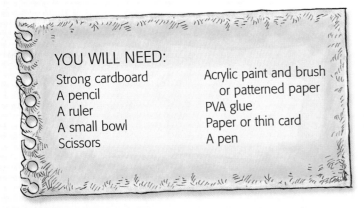

YOU WILL NEED:
Strong cardboard
A pencil
A ruler
A small bowl
Scissors

Acrylic paint and brush
  or patterned paper
PVA glue
Paper or thin card
A pen

STEP 3
Using a small bowl as a guide, draw a semicircle at the top of the cardboard rectangle and cut along it, to remove the corners. Then, towards the top of your cardboard shape, draw a circle that is about 5 cm wide. Cut it out to leave a hole.

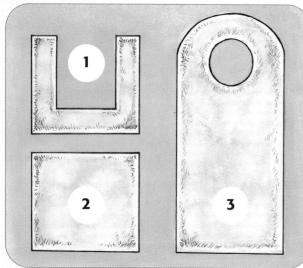

STEP 1
Use the ruler to draw two 12 x 12 cm squares and a 12 x 28 cm rectangle on the strong cardboard, and cut the three shapes out.

STEP 2
Take one of the cardboard squares and draw a vertical line 2 cm from each corner, and a horizontal line between them 2 cm from the bottom. Rub out the pencil lines in the bottom corners of the square, until you are left with a 'U' shape. Cut along the lines.

STEP 4
Paint the three cardboard shapes – the one shown here has a pirate theme.

STEP 5
Assemble the sign by glueing the U-shaped piece (1) to the back section (3). Then glue the square (2) on top of the U-shaped piece.

STEP 6
Let the glue dry, then write 'KEEP OUT!' in pen on a piece of paper. Slot it into the pocket you've created on the door sign.

CD Picture Cube

YOU WILL NEED:

2 CD cases
Photos or pictures
PVA glue

Cardboard
A pencil
Scissors

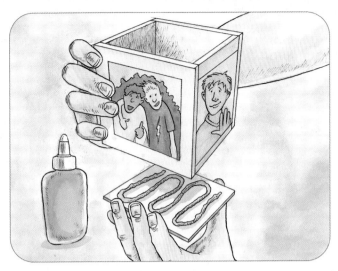

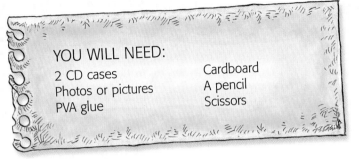

Display photos of your family, friends or dog.

STEP 1

Slip a photo inside the front part of each CD case.

STEP 4

Spread glue over the largest square. Stand the CD cube on top, lining up the edges and press it down firmly onto the glue.

STEP 5

Spread more glue over one side of the smaller square, then slip it down into the centre of the cube, pressing it down onto the large square base.

STEP 2

Stand the two cases upright, arranging them in a cube shape. Glue them together where their edges meet.

STEP 3

When the glue is dry, draw around the outside of the cube onto a piece of cardboard. On a second piece of card, draw around the inside of the cube. Cut out the two cardboard squares.

TOP TIP
Leave all the glue to dry, preferably overnight, before using your photo cube to stash stationery, hand-held games or other tiny treasures.

It's not just a photo frame – you can store things in it, too.

DEADLY CREATURES

What do the six critters described below have in common? They're all toxic hazards! From poisonous slime to killer saliva, they've got some of the nastiest habits on Earth.

HAIRY HORROR CATERPILLAR

The brown tail moth caterpillar is a furry fiend. It scoffs its way through trees and shrubs in spring, shedding its little hairs along the way. These hairs are horrid – they ride on the breeze and if they find a human to land on they prickle the skin, causing rashes, headaches and breathing problems.

HOME Europe and North America.

CHAMPION POISONER – THE BLACK WIDOW

The black widow's bite is one of the deadliest on Earth. It causes pain in all the muscles, followed by cramps, sickness and sleeplessness. It can take months for a victim to recover. Young children are at the greatest risk – as they're smaller, the poison affects them more. You don't have to go to the US or Canada to come across one of these spiders – they have been known to hitch rides in luggage as far as Sweden.

HOME United States and Canada.

UNPLEASANT PLATYPUS

The platypus may look cuddly, but it has a nasty little secret. The males have sharp spikes on the backs of their hind legs that deliver venom strong enough to kill a cat. If you are stung by a platypus, expect terrible pain. First the wound swells up, then the poison spreads along your limbs and your body slowly puffs up like a balloon. The pain is so bad, it can cause sickness or even fainting.

HOME Australia and Tasmania.

RELUCTANT STINGRAY

What would you do if you were lying around minding your own business and somebody stepped on you? This is a problem for the stingray, a flat, funny-looking fish that lives most of its life in peace on the sea floor. If a human foot lands on the ray who's relaxing, it quickly defends itself by whipping up its barbed tail and whacking it in the direction of the human's legs, injecting toxin through its barbs. It hurts a lot, but be reassured – death is rare. Just watch where you walk in warm shallow water.

HOME Warm coastal areas, such as Australia and the Caribbean.

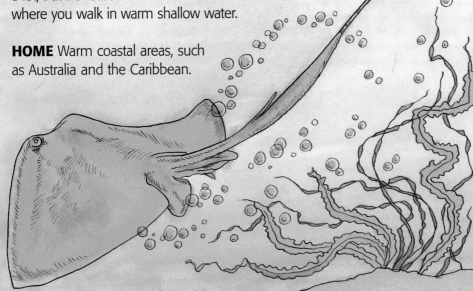

POISON ARROW FROG

Cute and colourful, these tiny frogs are the stars of the rainforest, but you wouldn't want to get too close as their skin is covered with a poisonous slime. Like many toxic terrors of the animal world, their poison is purely for defence. For centuries, people who hunt animals in the jungle have used the frogs' secretions to coat their arrowheads and poison their own prey.

HOME Central and South America.

SICKENING SHORT-TAILED SHREW

This sweet little rodent looks like it wouldn't harm a fly. But it wouldn't hesitate to hurt a slug, a frog or a newt. The shrew's saliva is an especially deadly kind of venom that paralyses – but doesn't kill – its prey. The cunning shrew can keep its captives fresh for up to five days, ready to chew on whenever it fancies. It can't kill a human, but it can certainly deliver a painful bite.

HOME North America.

DID YOU KNOW?

Venoms and poisons are both toxins – that is, stuff produced by plants and animals that causes harm to other plants and animals. The difference between venoms and poisons lies in the way they are delivered. Venoms are injected straight into the bloodstream (as in a snake bite), but poisons are transmitted through touch, or are swallowed.

CARD GAMES

POWER SWITCH

**The aim of this game is to get rid of all your cards.
You might think you know who is going to win – but there are some
crazy power cards that can change the 'state of play' quickly.**

Number Of Players: As many as you want, but use two packs of cards if there are seven or more players.

How To Play

Shuffle your cards (learn how to shuffle in style on the opposite page). Deal seven cards to each player. Put the rest of the cards face down in a stack on the table. Turn over the top card and place it next to the stack.

The player on the dealer's left starts. He has to play a card in the same suit (there are four suits: clubs, spades, hearts and diamonds) or with the same number as the turned over card. So, if the top card is a six of clubs, the player must play a six, or a club. If he can't, he must keep taking cards from the stack until he can. Then the game continues with the person on his left.

This is all straightforward, but beware – there are special 'power' cards. If a player puts down:

◆ A **two**. The next player is required to pick up two cards – unless he also plays a two, which requires the next player to pick up four. If that player plays another two, the next player has to pick up six. This sequence continues until none of the players has a two.

◆ A **seven**. The same player may play all the other cards they have in that suit.

◆ An **eight**. The next player misses their turn.

◆ A **black jack**. The next player must pick up five cards, unless he has a red jack – which cancels out the black jack. However, if he has the other black jack, the next player has to pick up ten (unless he has a red jack, in which case he doesn't have to pick up any cards and play continues).

◆ A **king**. The order of play changes direction.

◆ An **ace**. This can be played at any time. The person playing the ace can decide on the suit that must be put down next.

If the stack runs out during the game, take the pile of discarded cards (except the turned over card), shuffle it, and place it face down to become the new stack.

To Win

When a player is down to his last card, he must knock on the table loudly. If he doesn't, he can't play his last card on his next turn and has to pick up another card.

GO FISH

The object of this game is to collect all the cards of the same number, for example sevens or jacks. A good memory of who has which cards helps.

Number Of Players: Three to seven.

How To Play

The dealer deals five cards to each player. The remaining cards are placed face down on the table.

The player to the left of the dealer starts. He has to ask the other players for cards of a particular number – for example, sixes. The player must hold at least one card of the number he asks for. If the other players have cards of that number, they must give them to the asker. The asker then gets another go.

'Go Fish!'

If a player doesn't have any cards of that rank, he says 'Go Fish!'. The asker then has to pick up a card from the stack. If the drawn card is the number asked for, the asker shows it and gets another turn. If it is not the number asked for, the asker keeps it, and the turn passes to the player who said 'Go fish!'

The Book

When one player has all four cards of one number, they form a 'book', and are placed face up on the table. The game continues until either one player has no cards left in his hand, or the stack of cards on the table runs out. The winner is the player who then has the most books.

SHUFFLE IN STYLE

This is the 'Riffle Shuffle' – it takes some practice!

1. Split the pack approximately in half (there's no need to count the cards out). Take one half in your left hand, holding the top of the half-deck with your thumb and the bottom with your middle finger. Do the same to the other half of the deck with your right hand.

2. Hold the two half-decks face down and next to each other, just above a table.

3. Push the decks into a curve by pressing the knuckle of your index finger into the back of them. Flick the cards down on to the table; releasing them smoothly by curving your thumb slowly away. The cards should spring down so that, as cards from the left hand land on the table, cards from the right hand land on top. Continue until all the cards are on the table and mixed up.

4. Carefully lift up the two half-decks; one in each hand. Push the cards in slightly and then, resting your thumbs on the top of the decks, place your other fingers underneath and bend the decks upwards.

5. Finally, let go with your fingers and push down with your thumbs while pressing your palms inwards. The cards will spring together into one pack.

MONEY COUNTS

Turn your odd-jobbing talents into extra cash with this round-the-house chore scorecard.

Boys need extra pocket-money, and grown-ups need jobs done. Perfect: you'll do the jobs and your parents will pay. But beware – your parents might argue that you're supposed to help around the home. What you need to do is show them you are serious about helping out more – then they might change their minds. Here's how to do it:

1. Make a list of all the jobs people in your family like doing least.

2. Give each chore a score, or 'rotten-ness' rating from 1 to 10 (1 = a bit boring, 10 = the most horrible job of all).

3. Agree a fee with your parents for each job, based on its rotten-ness rating.

4. Write the jobs on a scorecard (like the one shown here), with a place where you can tick every time you complete a chore.

5. When the card is full of ticks just add up your score, then cash it in with the grown-ups – and start all over again.

What's washing the car worth in your family?

JOB	ROTTEN-NESS RATING	FEE	TICK
Cleaning out the rabbits' cage/cat litter tray	4	—	◯
Loading/unloading the dishwasher	2	—	◯
Weeding the garden	6	—	◯
Washing the car	6	—	◯
Vacuuming the house	3	—	◯
Polishing shoes	2	—	◯
Cleaning the kitchen floor	4	—	◯
Mowing the lawn	5	—	◯
Walking the dog	2	—	◯
Bathing the dog	10 (it's a stinky dog)	—	◯
TOTAL		—	

LARGEST BANKNOTE

The banknote with the largest currency amounts ever was the American $100,000 Series 1934 Gold Certificate with a portrait of President Wilson. These notes were never used for buying things. Banks used them for official business dealings. They were literally as good as gold because they could be exchanged for gold bars.

FOR BOYS WORLDWIDE, THERE'S NOTHING LIKE A POCKET FULL OF CASH. HERE'S WHAT YOU'D HAVE IF YOU WERE IN ...

CHINA

The Chinese invented many things, including the word 'cash', which means 'square-holed money'. That's because Chinese coins used to be made with holes in, so they could be carried around on a string. Today's Chinese money is called the Renminbi, meaning 'The People's Currency', and the main unit is the Yuan.

MONGOLIA

The Tugrug is the currency used in Mongolia. All the notes show Genghis Khan, a great warrior who created the Mongol empire. But Mongolians didn't always use notes. They used tea bricks – tea leaves mixed with ox blood and yak dung and pressed into a mould. It was light to carry and was believed to be a good remedy for coughs.

VENEZUELA

The currency of this South American country is one of the brightest and most colourful in the world. Its notes, called Boliívar Fuertes, come in a rainbow of colours and are decorated with beautiful pictures of famous Venezuelans on the front and animals that live in Venezuela on the back. These include such rare creatures as the American harpy eagle, the giant armadillo and the spectacled bear.

BRAZIL

The Brazilian currency is called the Real (or Reais for more than one). Inflation used to be really high in Brazil. This means that if one year a bag of sweets cost 10 Reais, the next year it might cost 1,000 Reais. When things got too much, the banks reduced the value of the currency and renamed it to make their economy work. They did this so often that today, 1 Brazilian real is equal to 2,749,025,730,000 (2.75 trillion) old Reais from 70 years ago.

DID YOU KNOW?

- In 2008, prices in Zimbabwe were going up so fast the government had to issue a 10 billion dollar note (yes, that's 10,000,000,000 dollars).
- Before 1971, Britain used a different currency with lots of funny-named coins. There was a half crown worth 30p, a shilling worth 5p and a farthing worth 0.1p. What would a farthing buy you today?
- There are loads of cool slang words for money – try using wonga, wedge, dough or dosh.

Have a Poop-Party

Freak out your friends by serving fudgetastic cowpats and chocolatey horse-dropping biscuits. Your mates will think you're udderly ridiculous when you eat one.

Warning: Have an adult help you when using the oven or hob. Remember to wear oven gloves when handling anything hot.

Cow Patties

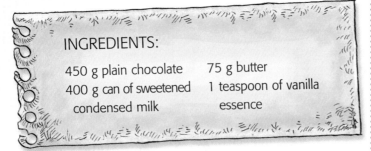

INGREDIENTS:

450 g plain chocolate
400 g can of sweetened
  condensed milk

75 g butter
1 teaspoon of vanilla
  essence

STEP 1

Line a baking tray with non-stick baking parchment.

STEP 3

Remove from the heat and stir in the vanilla essence. Allow to cool for 10 minutes, then beat well.

STEP 2

Break the chocolate into squares and place in a large saucepan with the condensed milk and butter. Heat gently, stirring constantly, until you have a smooth mixture. Do not allow the mixture to boil.

Flatten the dollops with the back of a spoon for the perfect cowpat look.

STEP 4

Using a tablespoon, place dollops of the chocolate mixture onto the baking tray. Use your artistic skills to make them look like cowpats. Chill in the refrigerator for at least an hour, or until set.

Chocolate Horse Droppings

INGREDIENTS:

115 g butter, kept at
   room temperature
75 g icing sugar
150 g plain flour
2 tablespoon of cocoa
   powder

50 g desiccated
   coconut
50 g milk or plain
   chocolate drops

STEP 4

Roll pieces of the dough into balls, about the size of walnuts, and evenly space the balls on the greased baking tray.

STEP 1

Preheat the oven to 180ºC/350ºF/Gas Mark 4. Lightly grease a baking tray by rubbing a little butter over the surface or brushing with a little vegetable oil.

STEP 2

Beat together the butter and sugar with a wooden spoon until light and fluffy.

Gently mix in the coconut so it doesn't lose it's flaky texture. White specks will give a realistic horse-poo effect.

STEP 3

Sift the flour and cocoa powder into the bowl and beat into the butter and sugar mixture. Stir in the coconut and chocolate chips. Using your hands, mix into a stiff dough.

STEP 5

Bake for 10 to 12 minutes, until just firm. Allow to cool on the tray for a few minutes, before transferring to a wire rack to cool completely.

53

Reading the Runes

Use 'runes' – letters of the Viking alphabet – to write your name, then make your own rune stones and find out how to use them to tell your fortune.

VIKING ABC'S

Vikings carved runes onto stone, wood or bone to mark their swords, rings, houses and other precious possessions.

The runes are listed below in the order of our alphabet. As well as representing sounds, like our alphabet does today, each rune had an ordinary meaning (listed below) and a magical meaning (listed below, in brackets). Fortune-tellers used these magical meanings of the runes to predict the future and cast spells.

A
ash
(information)

B
birch
(cleverness)

C
thorn
(protection)

D
day
(change)

E
harvest
(ending)

F
wealth
(survival, success)

G
gift
(shopping)

H
river fish
(happiness)

IJ
ice
(challenge)

K
torch
(shock)

L
water
(energy, mystery)

M
rushes
(power)

N
need
(duty)

O
mouth
(wisdom)

P
joy
(surprise)

Q
oak
(improvement)

R
riding
(journeys)

S
sun
(discovery)

T
warrior
(bravery)

UVW
cattle
(strength, speed)

X
home
(safety)

Y
axe
(defence)

Z
yew tree
(action)

RUNE MAGIC

Vikings believed that runes gave power to weapons and guarded against evil. They could reveal the future and also had the power to change it. Warriors before battle, leaders settling arguments and men with difficult choices to make all read the runes to guide and help them.

MAKE YOUR OWN RUNES

Gather together 23 small, smooth, pale-coloured, flattish pebbles – beach or garden pebbles are ideal. Then, take a black permanent marker pen – the type of pen used to write on CDs – and copy a letter of the runic alphabet onto each of the stones.

CASTING THE RUNES

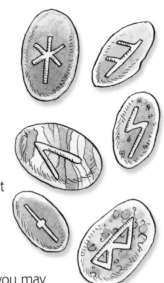

Put your runes in a handkerchief and shake them well. Scatter them onto a flat surface. This is called 'casting' the runes. Look at all the runes that land face-up and write down their magical meanings. These words might give you clues to what will happen in the future.

You can also use runes to help with a problem, wish or question you may have. Lay all the runes face down. Concentrating on your problem, wish or question, choose three runes. Turn them face-up and look up their magical meanings opposite. Write these meanings on a piece of paper and carry it around with you for a day. The three words should guide you towards action or help you find an answer, or show you what lies ahead.

WRITE YOUR NAME IN RUNES

Copy the letters of your name in runic symbols:

VIKING VANDALS

Rune writers were proud of their skills, so proud, they wanted to tell everyone. Vikings seeking shelter from a snowstorm carved graffiti-runes on the inside walls of the 3,000 year-old tomb at Maeshowe in Scotland. These weren't mighty words or magical spells. This is what they wrote:
'Haermund Hardaxe carved these runes.'
'The man who is most skilled in runes west of the ocean carved these runes.'

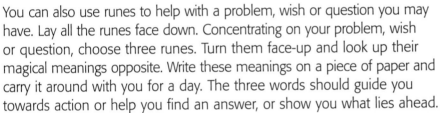

READ THIS WAY ➝

WHAT DO THE RUNES SAY?
Swords were often decorated with runic symbols. Can you work out the runes on this sword – running hilt to tip? Answer on page 61.

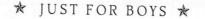

DRAW A SUPERHERO

YOU DON'T NEED ARTISTIC SUPERPOWERS TO DRAW ME. JUST FOLLOW THESE SIMPLE STEPS AND IN MINUTES YOU'LL BE FACE TO FACE WITH A COLOSSAL CAPED CRUSADER.

STEP 1

START BY DRAWING THE OUTLINES OF ALL THE PARTS OF THE BODY. LOOK HOW BIG THE CHEST IS - IT'S THE SAME SIZE AS THE SPACE BETWEEN HIS TWO FEET.

STEP 2

NEXT, DRAW HIS NEAR ARM WITH TWO OVALS AND A SMALL CIRCLE FOR THE HAND. MAKE SURE THE OVAL FOR THE UPPER ARM IS BIGGER THAN THE ONE FOR THE FOREARM.

STEP 3

NOW, ON THE OTHER ARM YOU CAN'T SEE THE UPPER ARM - SO JUST DRAW ONE LARGE OVAL FOR THE FOREARM AND A SMALL CIRCLE FOR THE HAND.

STEP 4

DRAW A LINE DOWN THE CENTRE OF THE BODY AND FACE. FOR THE MASK, ADD TWO LINES ABOUT TWO-THIRDS OF THE WAY UP THE FACE. DON'T FORGET THE LITTLE EARS.

STEP 5

PUT IN THE BOOTS, BELT AND CAPE WITH THEIR STAR SYMBOLS. ADD THE HAIR WITH SHORT, POINTED STROKES AND THE FINGERS WITH SHORT, CURVED STROKES.

STEP 6

TO ADD SHADING, HOLD THE PENCIL AT AN ANGLE AND PRESS SOFTLY. THIS WILL BRING OUT THE MIGHTY MUSCLES OF YOUR SUPERHERO. RUB OUT ANY MISTAKES WITH AN ERASER. FINALLY ADD COLOUR.

SUPERHERO JOKES

☞ Q. WHAT HAPPENED WHEN BATMAN AND ROBIN WERE RUN OVER BY A STEAMROLLER? A. THEY BECAME FLATMAN AND RIBBON!

☞ Q. WHERE IS SPIDERMAN'S HOME PAGE? A. ON THE WORLD-WIDE WEB!

Go Froggy

Frogs have been around on Earth for about 200 million years. They've had time to evolve some pretty cool habits, and some pretty weird ones, too.

THE LIFE CYCLE OF A FROG

1. Eggs
In Spring, frogs lay eggs in ponds. They can lay up to 4,000 at a time. Clumps of eggs are called frogspawn.

2. Embryo
Inside each egg, the frog cells begin to grow and develop into embryos.

3. Tadpole
The embryo eats its way out, and becomes a tadpole. It has a head, a mouth for eating, and a tail.

4. Back Legs
The tadpole starts to grow into a frog. First of all it forms tiny back legs.

5. Froglet
The tadpole grows front legs and lungs. Now it can breathe when it's out of the water. This is a froglet.

6. Adult Frog
When the froglet's tail drops off, it's finally a fully-fledged frog.

FANTASTIC FROGS

Freezing Frog

Most frogs like a warm home, but not the wood frog. These frosty fellows live in the Arctic Circle and stay buried and frozen solid underground for weeks. Their bodies form glucose – a kind of sugary antifreeze – which stops their organs icing up.

A Frog In The Throat

Darwin's frog is a type of frog that lives in the South American rainforest. It is named after the famous naturalist Charles Darwin. The male watches the eggs. As they hatch, he scoops them up in his mouth, where they live in his baggy chin. When they've grown into little froglets, they hop out, ready to make their own way in the world.

JOKE TIME
Q. What kind of shoes do frogs wear?
A. Open toad!

Eyes Down

Frogs don't have the teeth, or the muscles needed to chew food. They swallow their lunch whole, but the food gets stuck. So frogs help push food down their throats by sinking their eyes into their head when they eat.

Jumbo Jumper

Giant goliath frogs live by fast-flowing rivers in Cameroon, West Africa. Almost as big as pet cats (about 30 cm long), but with even longer legs, these amazing frogs are often hunted by collectors. Luckily their greenish-brown skin makes them almost invisible in the thick undergrowth.

Frogspawn Jelly

**Make your own edible clump of frogs' eggs.
This slimy, wobbling dessert is perfect for any spring party.**

INGREDIENTS:

1 packet of lime jelly
100 g plain or milk chocolate drops

Warning: Ask an adult to help you when boiling the kettle and pouring the hot water into the jug.

STEP 1

Break the jelly into cubes and place in a measuring jug.

STEP 2

Bring a little water to the boil in a kettle and, with the help of an adult, carefully pour about 100 ml of this over the jelly cubes. Stir until the jelly has completely dissolved.

STEP 3

Add cold water to fill the measuring jug up to 580 ml of jelly. Be sure not to add any more water than this or the jelly won't set. Allow to cool.

Add the chocolate drops before the jelly sets too hard.

STEP 4

Once the jelly has cooled, chill in the refrigerator until it begins to thicken. Then add the chocolate drops to the jelly and stir gently, making sure that they are evenly distributed.

STEP 5

Pour into a large dish. Place in the refrigerator for about two hours, or until it has set completely.

ANSWERS

COULD YOU AVOID THE PIRATES' PLANK? (pages 8–9)

6–10 points: Lousy Landlubber

Better brush up on those swimming skills for when they throw you overboard. The first mate's monkey would make a better pirate than you!

11–14 points: Captain Clever

You certainly have pirate potential. All that sucking up to the Captain should keep you safe, as long as the Captain's around. Beware! No one likes a clever clogs, so watch out for mutinous crew members.

15–18 points: Rotten To The Bone

You have certainly got sea legs. You were born to be a pirate. You know the pirate ropes – and what's more you know how to look after number one. Congratulations!

DIVE INTO THE DEEP

SPOT THE TEN DIFFERENCES (pages 12–13)

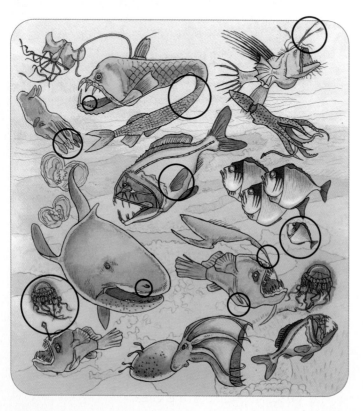

MATCH THE FISH DESCRIPTIONS (page 13)

1. Big, rubbery-lipped megamouth shark.
2. Poisonous, dome-headed jelly fish.
3. Leggy, pink deep-sea squid.
4. Flat, shiny-bodied hatchetfish.
5. Fanged, silvery-purple viperfish.
6. Yellow, long-spined anglerfish.

MIGHTY MAZE (page 17)

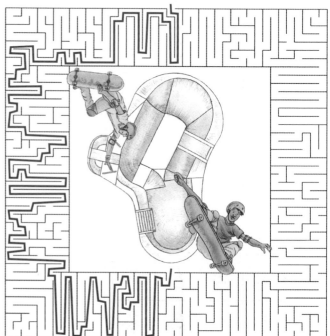

SUDOKU (pages 18–19)

BEGINNER

3	1	4	2
2	4	1	3
1	3	2	4
4	2	3	1

MEDIUM

3	2	1	4
4	1	3	2
1	4	2	3
2	3	4	1

KILLER

3	2	4	1
1	4	2	3
2	1	3	4
4	3	1	2

INSECT SUDOKU

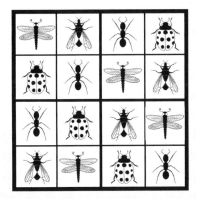

PIZZA PARTY

PIZZA NAMES (page 26)

Here is what you would get if you ordered:

b) Margarita   **d)** Hawaiian   **c)** Funghi   **a)** Pepperoni

MARVELLOUS MOTORS

WORD SCRAMBLE (page 36)

CAR SILHOUETTE GAME (page 36)

Limousine   Supercar   Pick-up Truck   Racing Car

WORDSEARCH (page 37)

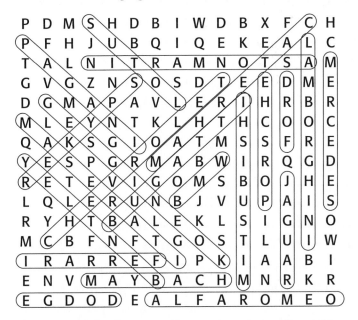

The name of the famous Italian supercar is *Lamborghini.*

READING THE RUNES

WHAT DO THE RUNES SAY? (page 55)

They read: King Canute The Great